Waving Goodbye to Parkinson's Disease

A Journey of Hope

By W. Stanton Smith
and Rosalind Lewis-Smith

Published by W. Stanton Smith LLC
Visit our website at www.wstantonsmith.com
Cover design and layout by Oleonmedia.
Library of Congress Cataloguing-in-Publicaton Data
ISBN: 978-1-4675-2549-7
Printed by Indexx Inc. in the United States of America
April, 2012

Contents

Acknowledgements

My sole purpose in writing this book in conjunction with my wife, Roz, is to give a realistic account of: 1) what has transpired since being diagnosed as a Person With Parkinson's (PWP); 2) the steps I've taken to restore my health to the greatest extent possible; and 3) my wife's role as Care Partner (CP) in this process.

My whole life has been prologue to my experience with Parkinson's Disease (PD). In this vein I am grateful to the many people have helped me throughout my life. However, I want to especially acknowledge my late mentor, Dr. Herry O. Teltscher. He was instrumental in providing the tools to change the way I looked at the world and thereby gave me a fighting chance to grapple with PD. Words fail to express how much I appreciate the positive role Herry played in my life. In addition I want to gratefully acknowledge Dr. Irving Dardik for his help and his selfless service to others.

As you will see in this book, I am blessed with an exceptional wife, Roz, who has always been at my side and shown resilience and loyalty way beyond the call of duty. She is the definition of a life partner and best friend and I am grateful to her beyond words.

In addition I have been given the gift of many concerned and loving friends and colleagues who have accompanied me on my PD journey. It is not feasible to name them all but you know who you are and I am very grateful.

Many, many thanks to Dominic Conde of Oleonmedia. His cover

design ideas are second to none as are his skills in laying out a book.

Another person deserving of a shout out is Dr. Mary Hughes, head of the Department of Neurology for the Greenville Hospital System (GHS). She has been most supportive of the efforts of the Parkinsons Support Group of the Upstate (PSGOTU) and my own objective to write this book. I might add that GHS is an impressive organization of people dedicated to serving the Greenville, SC community in a caring manner. It is a privilege to work with Dr. Hughes and this organization.

One final shout out goes to the leadership team at Deloitte LLP from which I retired as a principal. This team was supportive and accommodated my situation very creatively. I am very aware of how unusual this type of support is nowadays in business. Special thanks to Sharon Allen, Jerry Leamon, Barry Salzberg, and Jim Wall for their essential support.

W. Stanton Smith
April, 2012

Key Definitions
CP: Care Partner
PD: Parkinson's Disease
PWP: Person With Parkinson's

Introduction

Does the world need another book by a PWP? What is there left to be said? The answers: yes and plenty.

I was diagnosed with PD over 12 years ago. For the first six years my condition worsened significantly. For the past six-plus years my condition has improved dramatically. How did this happen? Can PWPs, their care partners (CPs), friends/relatives and other interested parties take away something helpful from my experience and that of my wife? I believe they can.

I intend this book to be a quick read that will motivate my fellow PWPs and their CPs as well as friends and families. By telling my story as a PWP and my wife telling hers as a CP, we hope very much that you will feel uplifted as well as learn something new that may help you.

Most importantly, we want you to: 1) realize that you are not alone in this struggle with PD; 2) be encouraged by the fact that a fellow PWP has found a way to make some progress against PD... something you can also do; and 3) be motivated to treat exercise as just as important as taking your medications on time and daily.

I also hope that health care professionals will read this and increase their understanding of how better to care for PWPs and CPs as well. This book will not go into great technical detail about the exercise program which has benefited me but there are references in the Appendix for those who want to delve more deeply into the details of *LifeWaves® Cycles Exercise®* Program.

W. Stanton Smith
April, 2012

Chapter 1
My PD Timeline – the first six years

It was the fall of 1999. I was looking out into a beautiful forest full of color from an office in suburban Connecticut. I'd changed jobs about 18 months before and was settling into this new opportunity. But something seemed seriously amiss. I was "stiff as a board," dragging my right leg and beginning to shuffle when I walked. My leg muscles, especially the quadriceps and hamstrings were so tight and often my equilibrium was so uncertain that when I stood up to leave my office, I was not steady on my feet. I hoped that no one would see me struggling.

I dreaded leaving the confines of my office. Once I started moving I thought that I looked and felt like the 1,000 year old man. But some days were better than others, so I tried to put it out of my mind. I told myself "just focus on doing this big job" I held as a principal in a global professional services firm.

When I got home, I was so exhausted that I often had to take a nap for up to an hour before I could even eat dinner. My wife, Roz, expressed concern about this seemingly endless fatigue. Finally the combination of exhaustion, shuffling around and putting my head in the sand was too much for Roz. She obtained a referral for me to see a local neurologist around my 51st birthday in December, 1999. It didn't take long for him to give a tentative diagnosis of Parkinson's Disease (PD) and prescribe some medication. I left the office unable to accept the diagnosis and completely in denial.

Determination is admirable but putting blinders on and not paying attention to what is reality is harmful to yourself and others. I learned that the hard way by trying to fake it at work. In my denial I thought that no one would pick up on my preoccupied manner, the shuffling, or the stiffness, or the increasing instances of briefly falling asleep during meetings. This fantasy world came crashing down at a meeting in Orlando, Florida in August 2000 about 9 months after the initial diagnosis.

It was time for the annual performance review of partners, principals and directors. Delivering the review was one of the two partners instrumental in hiring me. The review began with the words, "You're going to have trouble hearing this." By the end of the discussion it was clear that I'd fooled no one but myself.

Very much to the credit of the firm's leadership, a real effort was made to find a job I could do effectively. More importantly they were able to refer me to a highly respected neurologist in New York City. I recognize that many businesses would not have accommodated me. I will always be grateful for this support.

Once I was properly medicated and began acknowledging publicly that I had PD and that I was a Person With Parkinson's (PWP), life proceeded more smoothly.

I still worked long hours. As a consequence I exercised after 9 pm in the evening usually with a long walk around the neighborhood. I even was starting to do light jogging. Neighbors were inspired by my devotion to walking regardless of weather.

During this 18 month period, I began to feel as good as I had in years. The walking alone, getting a little extra rest and a job requiring less travel all seemed to be adding up to a reasonable accommodation to PD, at least in my mind. In fact I began to view PD as an annoyance and began to believe that I'd dodged a bullet. My tremors while evident were manageable, my stamina was improving with exercise and my outlook was about as positive as it had been in a while. The positive outlook I attribute to my continuing a meditation routine which calmed me down and helped get me in a more balanced frame of mind, as well as the unswerving support of my wife.

A false spring

This 18 month period proved to be a false spring. My neurologist had actually alerted me to the tenuous nature of my improved condition but I didn't focus on this cautionary counsel at the time. What he said was that any significant health related crisis could weaken me considerably and that it would be difficult for me to recover fully. He added that two such events might be too much for me or anyone to handle. I asked for clarification on "too much...to handle." His answer: "there would be a high probability of death." I was not reassured by this but I appreciated his candor.

In May 2002 the nature of this false spring became evident as a growth appeared on my neck. It grew into the size of a tennis ball. Thanks to the quick action of both my general practitioner and ENT, I was hospitalized and operated on by an extraordinary surgeon. I say extraordinary because what started as 30 minute procedure to drain an abscess became a 90 minute race to "vacuum up" an infection that had spread to just short of my brain and heart. The eradication of the infection required an 8 day stay in the hospital during which my PD meds stopped working completely. I would lie in bed shaking almost without respite with an IV in my arm and wondering what the next shoe to drop would be.

I continued working from my bed and then my home office. Due to an excellent staff reporting to me and support from my firm's leadership, as mentioned earlier, I was able to stay productive professionally. Thankfully my mental powers and stamina were not materially affected so I could continue to work albeit more often from home than before.

But there was one major consequence of this hospitalization. I could no longer walk any distance at all. My legs felt weak and my gait became halting. I started using a walker at home and a cane when I was out in public.

My motor skills began a noticeable decline. It took longer and longer to get dressed, to take a shower, to do anything that was physical. I could do little to help with household chores as I couldn't stand for very long and was unsteady on my feet when I was standing.

Another false spring

I now had descended to a lower plateau of life quality which lasted about two years. My frame of mind was beginning to be less positive. My wife had to assume increasing responsibilities for our life together. This was a strain for her that I could do little to ameliorate. This powerlessness to do my part preyed on my mind.

I threw myself into my work with what energy I had leaving little for anything else. Success professionally was at least keeping my focus on the positive aspects of life and diverting me from self-pity and general negativity which so often afflict those of us with PD.

On the brighter side, my physical condition had improved enough to travel with Roz to Venice for an international conference in the summer of 2004. I made a presentation about an innovative career guidance program which I'd played a major role in designing and implementing since 2002. I was feeling that I'd attained some modus vivendi with PD. This "truce" with PD would prove to be yet another false spring.

Yet another false spring

About 4 months later in November, 2004, my neurologist changed my primary medication due to new information that the medication I had been taking for the last 4+years had caused heart problems in enough cases to merit concern.

The transition from the old medication and onto the new was disastrous for my health. My reaction to the new drug made me bed ridden for about 8 weeks. I could not get out of bed without assistance.

With a full blown crisis on our hands, my wife set about to get a neurologist closer to where we lived in Scarsdale, New York. This turned out to be a good move as I was evaluated as under-medicated and in need of physical therapy.

Nonetheless I was fast becoming an invalid even though I was still able to do work from my home. Thanks to the help of a dedicated fitness trainer who visited me and stretched my legs once a day for nearly 2 months and a chiropractor who visited a couple of times a week to adjust me, and my Kinesiologist, I was able to very occasionally go to the office both in Manhattan and suburban Connecticut. However, the handwriting was on the wall. We had to prepare for me going on disability and doing so in a lower cost area.

Serendipity

It was June, 2005 when a serendipitous event occurred. Roz and I had scheduled a dinner in Manhattan with my 19 year old godson and a business colleague and her two college age children.

I was having a bad day…very stiff and shaking. With my discomfort very obvious to all at the table, my colleague's daughter asked if her "genius" uncle could help me. It turned out that one of his interests was a kind of interval training exercise program which had been of value to not just healthy people but also individuals with diabetes, MS and even cancer. My colleague agreed to ask her brother-in-law if he'd be willing to take my "case" on. She believed it to be a long shot but she'd ask.

Meanwhile Roz and I were looking at houses in the Greenville, SC vicinity. Any house that we liked was measured for a wheel chair. The episode with the medication change and adverse reaction had eroded nearly all my physical and psychological reserves. I was sinking fast.

As my condition seemed to worsen almost by the day, the words of my first neurologist came back to me. This episode with the bad reaction to new medication had constituted the second major health crisis from which it would be very difficult to recover. Put another way, this was strike two and for all I knew strike three was on its way and I was standing in the batter's box with no bat.

Meanwhile it was becoming difficult for me to get through meetings without nodding off or otherwise losing concentration. I began to wonder if I could do my professional work much longer even with the first rate staff that I had to support me.

Neither my wife nor I were happy about moving away from our supportive circle of friends but we felt we had no choice but to face the inevitable. Further, for the first time I began to feel angry at having run out of options and having to face succumbing to PD. While I was open to talking to my colleague's brother-in-law, I really was skeptical that there was anything practical that could be done to halt my evident decline much less improve my prospects for a better quality of life.

Chapter 2
Catching the *LifeWaves*® – the next six years

On a humid summer day in 2005 Roz and I had our first meeting with Dr. Irv Dardik. Irv explained the theory behind what has become "*LifeWaves*®*Cycles Exercise*® Program."

Interestingly, Irv spent most of his time talking to Roz. He was assessing whether or not Roz would be supportive of devoting myself to the program. His experience told him that without spousal support there was little hope that I would stick with the program.

Dr. Dardik explained that his original interest in interval training started when he was co-chair of the U.S. Olympic medical committee during the 1970s and the 1980s. It seems that many athletes became ill after ending their Olympic training and competitive regimens. He concluded that we were very good at training peak performance but we largely ignored the body's need to recover after challenging it to perform. As a consequence he developed the concept behind the *LifeWaves*®*Cycles Exercise*® Program to emphasize a balanced approach to exercise.

As Dr. Dardik explains it, traditional interval training specifies a specific time period for recovery and the next activity begins even if the body has not fully recovered from the previous activity. The *LifeWaves*® version of interval training doesn't prescribe a set length of time for recovery. In contrast readiness for the next activity is based on the heart rate returning or recovering to levels near where it started with the activity just completed. This way the body learns to be active when it needs to be active and rest when it needs to rest. This helps ensure that the "idling speed" is not unnecessarily high which can be a problem for PWPs in particular.

I am not going to go further into *LifeWaves®* details at this point. Those who are interested will find in the appendix a short exposition on what it feels like to experience the cycles within the program that I credit with profoundly improving my quality of life.

Here is the timeline of improvement from my starting *LifeWaves®* in August, 2005 to April, 2012.

Nearing the end of year 6 of PD diagnosis (summer of 2005), I could no longer:

• Tie my shoes.

• Tie a neck tie.

• Button a shirt.

• Reach for something without fear of falling forward.

• Walk without a walker or cane.

• Walk across a room without extreme concentration in order not to fall.

• Run or jog.

• Walk any distance without fatigue or danger of falling.

• Dress myself without major assistance.

• Stand in the shower.

• Stand long enough to put dishes in the dishwasher or wash/dry by hand.

- Stand at a kitchen counter or at a bathroom sink without holding onto the counter or sink top "for dear life."

- Write "large" or write legibly regardless of the size of the letters.

- Stand or sit with proper posture.

- Execute basic household chores like changing a light bulb or standing on a ladder.

- Concentrate for long periods of time.

- Easily make expressions with my face; I had the "Parkinson's mask."

- Go up and down stairs readily.

- Drive a car for more than 15 minutes comfortably.

- Sleep more than 4 hours per night.

- Sing for very long with control or proper breath support.

- Utilize a conventional knife, fork or spoon.

- Carry a full coffee mug or a glass of water safely

This is a long list of everyday activities that I could no longer do. When was the last time I couldn't do anything on the list above without assistance? The most likely answer is before age 5. The problem I had was that I had the awareness of someone in his early to mid-50s but with the motor capabilities of a pre-kindergartener…a desperate, claustrophobic feeling to say the least.

Had I made the right decision to start *LifeWaves*®? Had I sent myself and my wife on a fool's errand? Was I wasting our money? Could the quality of my life really improve? All these doubts assailed me. So I looked carefully to see if anything was improving.

I soon learned that while I didn't see gradual improvements, others did. And as they related their excitement at seeing these improvements, the more excited I became and the more convinced that I was on the right path for me.

Chronicle of improvements

So by the end of year 1 of LifeWaves® (August 2006), I was showing some noticeable improvement in mobility. People who hadn't seen me in months commented that I had more energy and better "color" in my face. Progress showed in enhanced flexibility, less spasticity and more alert behavior. This feedback made me increasingly hopeful.

By the end of year 3 (August 2008), I was able to walk without a cane or walker. I have a video of me jogging around a parking lot, walking unaided into an office and also tip toeing backwards in the same parking lot. By now I was beginning to believe that I might actually be able to turn things around with continued effort.

By the end of year 5 (August 2010), I was now able to do everything on the list above, perhaps not at the same level as prior to the PD diagnosis, but certainly adequately and without assistance nearly all the time. Now I had completely lost the sense of fear and desolation I had felt over the past ten plus years.

By year 6+ (April, 2012) improvements in mobility continue. I am now able to undertake activities that I haven't been able to do for ten years. For example:

• I am now able to walk up a steep road nearly three-tenths of mile long and rising 200 feet over that length. This road leads to the top of a ridge where we have a house. This feat is recorded on video and can be viewed on my website: www.wstantonsmith. com along with the videos of a June 2007 speech showing my condition after 2 years of LifeWaves® and the August 2008 activities detailed above.

- In addition to continuing the *LifeWaves®* program, I am now in a weight training program, having achieved enough physical capability to add this type of exercise.

Now here are some facts drawn from analysis of 6+ years of charting my heart rate:

- My average resting heart rate has lowered from about 100 beats per minute to about 80 beats per minute and moving into the 70s. This level is still higher than optimal but a significant improvement nonetheless. The goal is to get my resting pulse on average to be in the 60s.

- My heart rate variability is higher in the morning than in the afternoon which means that it is in sync with the circadian rhythms. This means that, among other things, my metabolism is functioning within a normal range now for the first time since the initial PD diagnosis.

Money matters

There is always the subject of what it costs monetarily to engage in a *LifeWaves®* or other high quality fitness program. I have had a number of conversations with PWPs who focus on the cost of fitness programs. Their concern is that devoting themselves to such a program will require both a time and money investment that many PWPs feel unable to undertake.

In the current difficult economic environment, I appreciate the need to scrutinize all expenditures. I also know for sure that the quality of my life and that of my wife have been greatly enhanced by my investing time and money in taking advantage of the tools I had access to such as *LifeWaves®*, kinesiology and neurologists. That said, when fellow PWPs say that they can't afford this level of investment in health, I reply, "How can you afford not to do it?"

I have also met PWPs who believe they are "too old" to begin a concerted effort at exercising. In my experience, I have observed PWPs and others with movement disorders benefiting from exercise, regardless of age or current physical condition.

A thought before moving on

In my opinion, being under stress continually and living without heeding circadian rhythms over a number of years contributed to my losing my health. The good news is that within a year of devoting time to *LifeWaves*® some relief occurred and year after year more improvements followed. Now by year 6+ much functionality has returned with the promise of more to come.

Do the 6+ years of grinding it out with *LifeWaves*® seem worth it? Yes! The remarkable improvements I've experienced with *LifeWaves*® make those years seem much, much shorter than the 6 years of continuous decline I experienced after the PD diagnosis.

Chapter 3
A Wife's Perspective as Care Partner

The care partner (CP) of a PWP also "has Parkinson's." Probably as stressful, if not more so, is being a part of the life journey of a PWP. This role of CP is one that is often overlooked. In this chapter, my wife, Roz, will reflect on how my being a PWP has affected her. She also gives some tips on how to cope with this role that truly no one "signed up" for.

The Diagnosis

When Stan went to the first neurologist in 1999, he went alone. BIG MISTAKE! I had to take his word for it that he "might have PD" and that the pills "might help." When the pills didn't agree with him, I couldn't persuade him to call the doctor back or to see him again, even when Stan's condition was clearly getting worse.

I insisted on going with him to the second neurologist (in New York City) to hear what the doctor said and to "keep Stan honest."

Following the second diagnosis, we both took PD seriously. I needed to know more about the disease, what my role would be, and what to expect in the future. So I bought several books on PD and sat down to read them. Another BIG MISTAKE! The books began with a list of all the horrible things that probably would happen to the patient with PD.

I never got past the first few pages. I became depressed, thinking about what our lives would be like, wondering when the next "stage" would happen. This dominated my thoughts for quite a while. Then I snapped out of it, realizing that there was no way of knowing exactly what would happen, or when. Stan had his challenges but he was OK for now. I threw away the books.

Beginning to Deal with PD

Stan was having difficulties not only with walking (he was dragging his right leg and his arm wouldn't swing freely), but also with fine motor control in his right hand. For some things he was able to use his left hand, but getting dressed was a slow and difficult process.

Being a good wife, I wanted to help him in every way. Stan said no, he wanted to do it all himself as much as he could. It was difficult watching him struggle with buttons and shoe laces, but it was the right thing to do. Neither of us wanted him to become dependent on my help.

The way I could help without doing it for him was to purchase some items to aid him in dressing: shoes with Velcro closings, a really long shoe horn combined with a hook to help lift clothing to the upper level in the closet. Other products are available, but these were the ones I chose for starters.

Stan was still able to do a number of household chores: he was able to go up and down stairs so he continued to do the laundry (I have arthritis in my knees) and he was able to clean up the kitchen after dinner. He also helped with grocery shopping.

Dealing with the "Crash"

Stan was stabilizing on the combination of the medication prescribed by the second neurologist and walking 30-45 minutes a day. Then came the "crash" when the neurologist decided to change his medication (there was new evidence of a problem with the first medication).

The process of weaning himself off the first medication and onto the second caused a "crash." Suddenly Stan's legs became weaker and weaker until after about a week he was confined to bed.

I was scared. It was terrible watching him struggle to move his legs. He was uncomfortable and I couldn't fix that. The second medication appeared to be causing a bad reaction. His neurologist was away and the one on call did not have a viable suggestion.

What could I do? I had no experience caring for someone who was helpless. I had no support group.

I purchased a walker. I lifted Stan's legs to get him settled in bed and to get him started walking when he got up. (Legs are really heavy!) I called Stan's chiropractor and he came over several times to help move Stan and get him up. Stan called his trainer and he came over to stretch Stan's legs and get him up and started walking.

Meanwhile, Stan wasn't taking any medication at all. The next thing I did was to insist that he see another (local) neurologist who had been recommended to me by a friend. It took several days to convince Stan to do this. I asked him just to go with me and make up his own mind which neurologist to continue with. (He decided on the new one after being prescribed a combination of medications and learning he had been under-medicated.) I had a stair chair installed so Stan could safely get down to the garage so I could take him to the neurologist.

Stan began to improve slowly with the new medication. I was tied to staying at home. I had to be on call 24/7. This was difficult for me, as I was used to a free schedule. Luckily I had already stopped working.

I called on a few friends who grocery shopped for us. I called on a couple of Stan's friends who came over and "sat" with him so I could go out. Eventually I was able to leave him at home as long as he had a phone nearby to call me if he got into trouble (he never had to).

Amazingly, Stan continued to work during this period. I brought his laptop to him even when he was confined to bed, and he had his cell phone to make calls. FedEx delivered papers he needed. Most of his staff were in other states and he already worked with them over the phone and via email.

The period of the "crash" lasted nearly two months and exhausted me. I wished I had had a PD support group to talk to, but I didn't really know of their existence. Now I know that if anything like this ever happens again I would hire a home care service to help me out. I just didn't know where to turn.

Recovering from the "Crash"

Stan became able to walk with a cane instead of the walker. He wore sweatpants and T-shirts around the house so dressing wasn't a chore. Of course, he no longer could help with laundry and cleanup. After about two months he needed to go to the office so I drove him (about 1½ hours round trip).

Stan was having trouble managing a fork and knife. I began cutting up his food for him, and eventually I cut things (like chicken) into bite-size pieces before cooking it. I used short pasta shapes like penne rather than strands like spaghetti or linguini. I bought eating utensils with large, weighted handles that were easier for him to manage. I bought lightweight plates and bowls that he could carry back and forth from kitchen to table, and plastic glasses. I looked for anything that would help him feel more independent.

Stan began driving himself to work when he needed to be in the office, but it was difficult for him. He still worked at home as much as he could. The situation was far from ideal.

Moving to South Carolina and Beginning *LifeWaves*®

Five months after the "crash" Stan wanted to move to South Carolina for warmer temperatures. The cold causes his legs to tighten up, and snow and ice are treacherous to walk on. He still wasn't very stable and needed his cane all the time. We thought he was headed for a wheelchair. So, when we looked at houses in SC, I measured doorways for wheelchair access.

One month before we closed on our new home, Stan and I met with Dr. Irv Dardik to learn about *LifeWaves*®. It was a fascinating meeting. Dr. Dardik explained that he believed the system could help with PD, and had conducted a 16-week research study with PD patients a few years earlier which gave some indication that it could help. Stan took a leap of faith and decided to sign up for the program. At this point he was so frustrated with his condition that he was willing to try any reasonable approach.

Little did I know that Dr. Dardik was interviewing me as well as Stan. We found out later that he would not have agreed to start Stan on the program if he had not felt that I was supportive and would not interfere with Stan's staying on the program.

Progress and the Breakthrough

We purchased a stationary bicycle for Stan to use for the exercises; he also used the staircase as an alternate method. Staying on the exercise schedule was a challenge; as it took up to an hour every other day However, Stan managed to organize his work around the exercise schedule, even when he had to travel back to NY for meetings.

Progress was slow. Changes in Stan's stability were barely discernible for a long time. He had to grab onto the kitchen countertop to avoid falling when he lost his balance. Stan was feeling better, though.

Sometimes when you see someone every day, it is difficult to see the changes. But our friends in NY could see the improvement in Stan, as they only saw him every six months or so.

After a while Stan reduced his dependence on the cane. One day about four years after Stan started *LifeWaves*®, we were walking down a hallway and I was several steps behind him. He had his cane with him but he was not using it. All of a sudden I realized that he was walking evenly, not limping or dragging his right leg. I stopped him and hugged him, telling him what I had just seen. (By the way, hugging him standing up is usually a "no-no," as it can cause him to lose balance and possibly fall.)

Around the same time, because his balance had improved, Stan began to do the dishes and load the dishwasher after dinner! To this day, he always cleans up the kitchen. To me, that was a great victory.

How It Is Now

I no longer worry about him constantly, but it is always somewhere in my mind that Stan has PD. I trust him to know whether he is feeling well enough to drive (he limits his driving to 45 minutes). If we are going somewhere together I always do the driving.

There are times when Stan has problems walking or standing up for a period of time (like first thing in the morning). However, he knows if he climbs a set of stairs once or twice, his legs will loosen up and he will be almost back to "normal."

If he is dressing in a hurry I will help him with collar buttons and straighten the shirt collar after he puts his tie on.

He no longer needs the special utensils to eat, although he still uses the lightweight plates most of the time.

For a while, the side effects of some of his medication caused him to have nightmares, but he has been able to adjust his dosage and that rarely occurs now.

People we have known for a long time still marvel at how well he looks. I'm happy to say that now I am used to it!

A Final Word

There will be times that CPs will need help. I would suggest joining a support group even if you don't feel you "need" one now. You will make friends in the group and will be able to turn to them for support when you are in need.

Accept help when it is offered by friends or neighbors if you need it. For example, we have neighbors who will help with some household chores that we are unable to do (such as change overhead light bulbs or carry heavy objects). In times of extreme need you may receive offers to grocery shop or even provide meals. Their offers are sincere and heartfelt and they want to help you.

Chapter 4
Eye Witnesses-what to expect from those who observe you

If you've ever been eye witness to an accident of some seriousness, you know that it leaves images in your mind that can be lasting. A welter of conflicting emotions sweep over you…fear, revulsion, a desire to help, confusion, a desire to deny the reality of what you just saw…to name just a few.

As PWPs we are witness to the "train wreck" which is PD while also being witness to the many and varied reactions that we see on the faces of those who observe us. We see faces reflecting concern and kindness countered by faces reflecting contempt, fear, and irritation at us moving slowly or just looking "deformed."

For some of us PWPs the final indignity of PD is the reaction of others to our appearance. If we followed our feelings sometimes we'd just avoid public contact to avoid the discomfort or even humiliation.

In my experience that only adds to the pain a PWP feels. For our own sanity we must continue to live in the world as we find it. To help PWPs and CPs deal with "eyewitnesses," I've developed four expectations or the four E's. Through the four E's I've tried to capture what to expect from others and what can be done by PWPs and CPs to remain positive.

The Four E's

Expect a visceral reaction of fear and even disgust from some people. Take this as an opportunity to educate them.

Speechless in Greenville

At a large PD Symposium in April 2011, the crowd of PWPs, CPs and health professionals was beginning to leave the main event room of the Convention Center. One of the Boy Scouts assigned to help anyone in need stood near me as I watched over the Parkinson's Support Group of the Upstate information table. His eyes were bulging out of his head. He tried several times to talk but his mouth could only open part way and no sound emanated.

Finally after much of the PD community had exited, he summoned up the courage to speak. He asked, "How do you catch Parkinson's?" There was real fear in his facial expression. I asked, "Are you freaked out by what we with Parkinson's look like?" He nodded yes. "And you're afraid that you could catch this disease by being in contact with us?" Another nod yes. I said, "you can relax because PD is non-communicable…you can't catch it from someone else."

He looked relieved and walked away to help the PWPs and CPs as requested. Later, a fellow PWP and I rode down the elevator with this scout and another. My fellow PWP is a tall imposing man. He smiled and looked at the scout and his buddy and asked, "are you going for Eagle Scout?" They both nodded yes. My fellow PWP then said, "I was an Eagle Scout too. In fact the youngest in the state ever at that time."

My scout who seemed to be handling this encounter so well to this point suddenly had a relapse. Learning that my fellow PWP had been an Eagle Scout seemed to fill him with terror all over again. He and his buddy acted as if they were trying to become a part of the elevator wall. When the door opened, it was a "jail break" as they left the elevator as fast as they could.

My fellow PWP and I were amused. However, this is a microcosm of how some may react to those of us with PD. This type of reaction can be hurtful unless we develop a sense of humor and a readiness to educate others about PD.

Expect friends, especially at first, to be uncomfortable around you and even avoid you. Take this as an opportunity to show understanding and reach out to them.

Avoidance of situations which make us uncomfortable is natural. So expect it and realize that friends and colleagues are struggling too just like the Boy Scouts above.

What follows is a good friend's story in his own words about his struggle to accept PD's impact on me:

Scott Salik – long time friend

I have known Stan Smith since the early 90's, well before he was showing the obvious signs of Parkinson's. The length of our friendship has allowed me to experience the before, during and after of his evolution of the disease.

Since I only see Stan from time to time, the changes in his mobility were obvious with each visit. I am not proud of the fact that I found it difficult to see the deterioration of his body, and at first would try to shorten the time of each interaction with him. But there came a point where I started to see beyond the physical signs and realize that it was the same old Stan behind the costume of Parkinson's.

The great part of getting to that point was that I was able to experience his miraculous devolution of the disease's evil symptoms. When the disease set in he always needed help to get around. You could see him carefully planning his path across the room. He would spot the points in the room where he could pause to get his footing, or take a rest, or catch himself if he began to fall. Even when he relied on his cane, when I was around Stan, I always was prepared to catch him.

Then a funny thing happened. You could see he made less planning in his path, less worry about his stability and less reliance on the cane. With each visit life became less of an issue for Stan and he would volunteer to get something if someone needed it. And then, poof even the cane was gone, and his footing became surer and more stable. I would even say that there are days now when I forget he even has Parkinson's.

Pretty amazing results for the hard work he has done on this new therapy. Not to mention how inspiring the evolution has been.

Expect others to be watching how you handle PD. Realize that you can impact others (for better or worse) by your example, especially younger people.

Here are representative examples of eyewitness statements from two young people under 30 to give you a flavor of the principle I'm illustrating.

Joe Zakierski – mentee

Stan is a true career facilitator. I was able to witness firsthand his ability to connect colleagues with each other in order to improve the overall organization and its individuals. He is an incredible role model for people with Parkinson's and other types of diseases because of how much he has achieved since being diagnosed. He has helped me understand that with hard work and determination – anything is possible.

Kiira Benzing – business colleague

While working on my documentary film, The Wave Maker, a film about Dr. Irving Dardik, I met Stan Smith. It was the fall of 2008 and Stan had been on LifeWaves® for about 3 years. Just before his interview he had done the exercises for that day. We then proceeded to film Stan for an hour and a half. Throughout the interview I noticed Stan's right hand tremble consistently. During the interview Stan mentioned that if he concentrated on making the trembling stop he could, and as he spoke this, his hand stopped trembling. We filmed Stan getting dressed as he readied himself for a business meeting; and his right hand functioned in aiding him.

About two years later I flew down with my crew to film Stan at his home residence. Surprising to me, Stan's stride had improved and I noticed far less trembling in his hands. Stan carried on doing daily activities like driving, walking, writing, and attending choir rehearsal. I also listened to Stan sing opera and I was amazed at the vocal range he exhibited. Stan's perseverance and optimism should be inspiration to us all; and I look forward to including his story in my film.

Expect others to want to help you but not know quite what to do. Take this opportunity to connect with them by accepting help while also letting them know when you won't accept help.

My experience is that it is important to be clear about when we PWPs need help and when we need to do it ourselves so we can maintain physical capability and sense of self-esteem. We PWPs understand that there is no worse feeling than having a sense of helplessness and dependence. On the other hand I've learned to see the love behind gestures to help even if they aren't welcome sometimes. As in all matters in life, a balance is required between stubbornly believing that we can do things that any observer knows we can't do any longer and becoming a drag through total dependency on others.

You may ask, "how do you show that you are willing to help but sensitive to PWP's or CP's feelings at the same time?" I'll answer it by giving the example of a neighbor of ours currently. He has made it clear that he will do any housekeeping chore such as changing lights bulbs or alarm system batteries or carrying a heavy box down stairs or run an errand. He is never insistent but is persistent by frequently asking what he or his wife can do to help.

A logical follow up question is, "Then what are the most useful actions you can take to help out a PWP and/or CP?" The answers are: 1) anything that gives the CP a break from being constantly vigilant. It could be giving the CP some time to do some shopping or go to the hair dresser or just take a nap or play a round of golf. It is important for the CP to be able to do something for himself/herself on a regular basis. Otherwise fatigue and resentment can build to dangerous levels; 2) anything that helps maintain some orderliness and cleanliness in the home or other space in which the PWP and CP are living; and 3) provide transportation to doctors, place of worship or venues outside the home.

One final tip to PWPs and CPs. Make a list of what tasks would be helpful when you need help. Each time someone asks how they could help, give them this list and tell them to choose the one (or more) they'd like to do. Everyone likes to feel that they have choices and this give them that chance.

A thought before moving on

Take a look at the appendix for more eyewitness accounts. I've included them not only to offer more proof of my improvement but to suggest a model for how you can keep track of your progress on all fronts. I've found that friends are willing to tell you the truth if you ask and you are receptive to input.

I realize that retreating is what we PDs feel like doing much of the time. However, humans are not intended to bear burdens alone. Trust that others, not everyone but enough, will respond if you reach out. This will ease your journey.

Chapter 5
A Word of Encouragement

I hope that I've whetted your appetite to further investigate ways to take more control of your destiny. PD can rob us PWPs of our sense of confidence leaving us with a sense of futility, hopelessness and frustration. I believe that my experience provides hard evidence that PD's progress can be dramatically slowed and quality of life vastly improved by taking the right steps to exercise properly as well as to develop a positive mindset.

As a parting word of encouragement I'll leave you with six thoughts that I hope you'll keep in mind as you continue to struggle with PD (whether you're a PWP or CP). These 6B's are:

Be knowledgeable about PD but not obsessed with how bad it could be. Live in the "now."

Be compassionate towards yourself and those close to you.

Be active, determined and optimistic as you fight your condition.

Be a lifelong "unlearner" as well as learner.

Be committed to exercising consistently in a variety of ways to keep you interested and motivated.

Be active in a Parkinson's support group.

I hope that you've seen how willpower can trigger improvement that is substantial if you choose to exert your willpower. Living the 6B's creates a positive wave of energy that builds on itself and makes physical progress much more likely.

Be knowledgeable about PD but not obsessed with how bad it could be. Live in the "now."

When I was diagnosed with PD, my wife purchased many books related to the disease. She began to read them avidly and reported to me what she found. The result was depression and a sense hopelessness that began to overtake us. There was an air of inevitability that was essentially paralyzing.

To have simply stopped reading the bad news would have been to continue the denial process. On the other hand to have continued to feel hopeless and depressed was unacceptable also. So we reached for a middle way which was to educate ourselves as to the condition in order to create a basic framework within which to operate. This approach accepted the facts that PD is a degenerative disorder and that certain "bad" things would more than likely happen over time. However, there was no need to sit and wait for these bad things to occur. We learned to acknowledge the facts and get on with living life as best we could.

Be compassionate towards yourself and those close to you.

As PWPs and CPs know, PD is a disease with clear outward signs. As a result everybody we come in contact with is affected…the clerk in a store who sees you moving uncertainly through the aisles…a friend who asks with concern whether or not you can negotiate a set of stairs…the individuals who help you through the airport security screening…your spouse or partner who may have to do chores around the house because you can only stand up for short periods of time if at all or don't have the steadiness of hands to even use a knife in order to cut a piece of fruit…all these "others" in your life either are filled with some anxiety and/or assume extra duties because of your condition. This naturally can lead to others feeling put upon even while feeling sympathetic towards you. Further, all the inconveniences can lead to resentment, anger and generally a negative environment at home.

What's a reasonable solution for all concerned? On my part it was developing a sense of gratitude to others for accommodating me…friendship must be accepted as a gift from others. On the part of others who interact daily with PWPs, I would ask for some forbearance on your part. Why? We PWPs sometimes freeze and don't respond immediately even if we want to do so. Patience oils what could be unrelenting friction between those who are *able* and those who are *disabled*. Nevertheless no one has to put up with moodiness on the part of a PWP.

I recognize the reality that many a relationship falters under the strain of PD. CPs and other family and friends can wind up feeling put upon. The phrase often used by CPs who are "bailing out" is "I didn't sign up for this."

Sounds reasonable but I've come to the conclusion that whenever I am tempted to use the phrase "I didn't sign up for this," I find that I am avoiding responsibility for my life. Something good, even great, can come out of adversity but it requires a willingness to find the learning point in every situation. I ask myself, "What is the situation teaching me and how can I activate my reasoning power, willpower and activities to do the right thing for all involved?" Without objectivity, I become angry, resentful and closed off from others, lost in self-absorption. It is not "fun" to acknowledge how I've contributed to a negative situation but there is no forward movement without a commitment to the truth about my role in every situation in life.

Life truly is what happens while we are making other plans. If I bloom where I'm planted the odds of a more satisfying life substantially increase. An added benefit is that others will be glad to be around me as I'll be a point of light in their lives.

Be active and optimistic in choosing to fight your condition.

This is a tall order as you feel yourself slowing down, getting tighter physically, unable to do simple motor actions like button a shirt, much less complex actions like play a sport or engage in an enjoyable pastime like singing in a choir.

I found that extreme emotional swings would occur from feeling that I could handle PD to absolute despair when I was in a hospital bed being treated intravenously for an infection with none of the PD medications working or even more intensely as I was lying in an easy chair unable to stop shaking during an adverse reaction to a change of medication.

All these feelings of despair and frustration were very real but I was determined not to let them rule me. I used my practice of meditation and affirmations to get me off the "floor" and get back to some functionality. To survive I realized that I had to "spiritualize" my life.

What does spiritualizing my life mean to me? The answer comes in two parts. Firstly, I've learned that humans are basically goal seekers. We have a desire and we work to obtain the desired thing. It follows that an effective tool to build a more satisfying life on all levels is to set a positive stretch goal.

Secondly, I define religion and spirituality as differing concepts but with some overlap. Religion unfortunately is too often associated with hierarchy and dogma, and a perceived tendency to exclude. In contrast spirituality connotes a tendency to include, and an awareness of the interconnectedness of all. This in turn leads to recognition that we are a part of a greater whole and that we live together most harmoniously when we keep each other's best interests at heart.

Be a lifelong "unlearner" as well as learner

Along the way I've learned to "unlearn." This is no easy feat and I must constantly work at it. For example, I would have been unable to see the possibilities in *LifeWaves*® were it not for unlearning the limiting, cynical thought processes that I once strongly held. In the process of developing a world view of my own, I had to unlearn negative self-talk, raging about how I was being treated by others, and always expecting something to go wrong.

What is unlearning? Unlearning consists of two steps. The first is stopping a behavior or thought process and forgetting how to repeat it in the future. The second step is to replace the unlearned behavior with a positive behavior. In my case I worked to replace a cynical, suspicious outlook on life with a positive set of values which helped me help myself out of binds I get myself into. It gave me some precepts by which to avoid old negative patterns and increased my chances of having a fulfilling life despite PD.

Focusing on PWPs specifically, unlearning means dropping all the negative mantras like "why me?" "I didn't sign up for this," "I can't change," "It's too hard to push myself to be physically active," "What's the use?" and "Why can't I swallow a pill and be cured?"

What replaces these mantras? The void is filled with mindfulness, i.e., paying attention to the little successes in a PWP's life such a tying a necktie even if it takes 5 minutes now or buttoning a shirt even if it takes much more time than it used to. Mindfulness means acknowledging improvements and paying attention to the details of life. This keeps your mind active and alert to the many opportunities to enrich your life.

Mindfulness also includes paying attention to how your medications affect you. Some PWPs complain that neurologists don't warn them of a side effect or what to expect from the medication or what the next down turn might be like. Perhaps the neurologist didn't meet patient expectations but to be balanced about this, neurologists face several conundrums: 1) they see a patient infrequently and have no way of knowing if the patient is a having a good or bad day unless the patient tells them; 2) patients may not share the details of how they are reacting to medication; and 3) neurologists often are not kept in the loop about major life events like being hospitalized for some condition unrelated to PD. Such an event could have an indirect impact on a PWP's PD symptoms that the untrained eye would not see.

Human nature seems to be to talk to everyone but the doctor about problems encountered with treatments prescribed by a doctor. You can help educate your neurologist and create a team approach to your care. I'm pretty sure that he/she will appreciate it and you'll be doing yourself a favor.

Apropos of learning and unlearning, here is an eyewitness statement from my current neurologist. It shows that you can help your neurologist learn something new to the benefit of you, your neurologist and his/her other patients (whether or not they are PWPs).

John F. Pilch MD-neurologist

Stan's story is a remarkable one which I have witnessed the past six years. His diagnosis of Idiopathic Parkinson's Disease dates back to the 1990s. While his signs and symptoms have been typical, the changes in Stan over the years have been anything but. Rather than worsening, his functional capability has actually improved! The most striking feature has been his smooth, deliberate voice. So what is his secret? He sings regularly and has the commitment to fitness of a professional athlete. Research suggests exercise can actually improve the structure and function of the brain and Stan has me believing it.

Be committed to exercising consistently in a variety of ways to keep yourself interested and motivated in improving your health.

For me exercise goes beyond the physical workouts to improve mobility et al. It encompasses keeping my voice in shape. Earlier in my life I had extensive voice lessons and I depend on what I learned then to assist me in this regard. In addition I sing in a choir and have along the way created a CD or two of Broadway songs with limited distribution to friends and colleagues. The purpose is not just creative expression but to track the health of my voice.

You say that you couldn't carry a tune in a bucket. Perhaps but if you can sing at all I urge you to sing. There is research that indicates that PWPs who sing have a greater sense of wellbeing and even experience a decrease in tremors. If you really can't sing, I suggest the LSVT Loud speech treatment therapy as one that will help you cope with the deterioration of vocal capability which all of us PWPs experience. (For more information go to www.LSVTGlobal.com)

I also urge my fellow PWPs to make interval training a continuing part of your life. Why? Because it provides a proven approach toward exercise which is anti-inflammatory and as we PWPs know "swollen," inflamed," and "stiff" are three words which describe our condition all too well.

Yes, any kind of exercise will help you feel better but the innovative type of interval training I've undertaken can help make you better. *LifeWaves®* training is designed to create "health," i.e., helping the body reverse course and move towards whatever being healthy would look like if you were your age without PD. But this reversal towards health is not an overnight process. There must be on-going dedication and commitment. With these two attributes as a base to work from, the PWP has the tools to make life with PD increasingly reasonable.

To my mind, there is also a direct correlation between devoting myself to *LifeWaves®* and a turnaround in the notable deterioration of my vocal capability. The quote below is from **Dr. John King**, Minister of Music at Hitchcock Presbyterian Church in Scarsdale, New York. It is Dr. King's take on the impact of interval training on my voice.

I have known Stan Smith for over 20 years. When I met him, he was a picture of good health. After he was diagnosed with Parkinson's, I watched his health deteriorate over the years. His hand tremors became more severe and he became less and less mobile. I even noticed a decline in his singing—his voice did not have the same control or range. However, since he has started his current regimen, I have noticed a miraculous turn around. I spent time with him recently, and I observed that his hand tremors were almost undetected, his step was virtually without stagger, AND his singing voice more focused and supported.

If you still believe that interval training is not a feasible path for you, there are other ways to stay active and have fun. Nintendo's Wii video game products (baseball, tennis, bowling, and other activities) can involve not just you but family members in entertaining and useful physical exertion. In addition Pilates classes and other regimens which require focused and controlled movement such as Hatha Yoga and Tai Chi increase your powers of concentration and mobility.

I have also found chiropractic treatments to help. Special mention is in order for Kinesiology which my chiropractor has utilized in treating me over the years, in particular the first six years of my PD diagnosis. (If you are interested in learning more about what Kinesiology can bring to the table, please consult my website, www.wstantonsmith.com and the transcript of an interview that I conducted with Dr. Robert Frey about how he treated my PD.)

So when all is said and done, don't wait for a pill to cure PD. If it comes, great but in the meantime, take steps to assertively improve your health. I can attest that when you see the very positive improvements from a concerted effort to physically exercise, in my case interval training, your outlook on life will improve substantially… to say nothing about the improvements in your physical health that you'll experience.

Be active in a Parkinson's Disease support group

A PWP colleague once told me that a doctor had advised him not to join a support group because it was "just a group of people crying on each other's shoulders." Putting aside the offensive emotional "tone deafness" that this statement conveys, I would say this is a perception that holds back PWPs, CPs, family members and concerned friends from availing themselves of a source of much needed support.

Another belief that holds back PWPs and CPs is encompassed in a statement made to me by a PWP. He said, "I'm young onset and I don't want to see what I'm going to look like in a few more years. It's too depressing!"

My recommendation to both of these PWPs was that they attend support group meetings and compare and contrast their mental states before and after attending a meeting. I stated my belief that they were cutting themselves off from a source of emotional strengthening as well as information which would be very helpful to them.

PD is hard enough to contend with without adding isolation from others to the list of negative disease-related events in your life. Remember that humans are social beings. We are meant to be together, and interact. As mentioned earlier the body itself needs interaction in order to function properly much less our psyches.

If there isn't a support group in your area, take the initiative and start one. It need only be an hour over coffee and cookies at your home or in a room at a community center. The agenda can be simply each person talking about their experiences and learning from each other. If this is crying on each other's shoulders, then let the crying begin because support groups are proven to help participants cope with serious life issues.

Of course such a support group if successful will grow to where you can have guest speakers to talk about a variety of topics that are germane to PD. The support group we belong to (The Parkinsons Support Group of the Upstate) also has peer group meetings which are facilitated by trained professionals. There is one group for PWPs and a separate one for CPs. The feedback is that it is a relief to be able to talk about the wrenching changes that occur in your life when you are diagnosed with PD, and, most importantly, to realize that you are not alone…you are not the only one who feels the way you do.

Is a support group a crutch? I'd say yes and what's wrong with using a crutch if that's what reality calls for? If you have a broken leg, but could walk if you had a crutch, why would you refuse to use the crutch? To resist help which is available is simply continuing the denial of the seriousness of the disease condition.

Concluding thoughts

My goal has been to show that there are tried and true tools for PWPs (and sufferers of other major diseases for that matter) to deal effectively with their condition. I have shared my experience with the LifeWaves®Cycles Exercise® Program as an example of an exercise program which can turn your life around if you commit to it. In addition we've offered a CP's perspective on PD.

Ironically PD has been one of the best things to happen to me because it made me focus my energies, opened me up to the high level of goodwill that humans are capable of, showed me what a miracle the human body is and what impressive results can be produced by the mind when concentrated on a positive outcome. My hope is that the contents for this book have inspired you, whether you are currently ill, or are in perfect health, to a new level of respect for what we each can achieve if we align our reason, will and determined activity to achieve a worthwhile goal.

Appendix

More details on the *LifeWaves®Cycles Exercise®* Program

Here are the basic aspects of the program that I have been following over the past six plus years.

Principles of the program

- Devote one hour every other day for three weeks out of the month and twelve months out of the year, with the fourth week of each month being a week of "recovery."

- Exercises are of brief duration. There are 4-7 exercise sets each no more than 2 minutes in length. After each brief exercise there is an interval of recovery which at a minimum lasts 3-5 minutes.

- The exercises are relatively easy to do as the goal is wake up the body's memory of how it performed when it was healthy, i.e., give the body a taste of success and the opportunity to accustom itself to that success.

- Align heart rate variability with naturally occurring cycles (also known as circadian rhythms) i.e., active during the daylight hours and less active at night. Train the body in time windows, 6-9 am, 9 am-12 noon and 3-6 pm. Lessen activity between 12-3 with a 30 minute nap.

- Train the body that when it is active, it shows it and when it is supposed to rest that it rests. Heart rate variability is naturally higher in the morning to get you going and less in the afternoon to sustain peak activity.

• Target sleeping 8 hours per night with getting up once during the night expected.

By following the program assiduously, a pattern of improved health should emerge.

Why the program works

To understand how this pattern of improved health occurs, Dr. Dardik explained to Roz and me some fundamental patterns found in all living organisms. The most noticeable of these patterns is what is called the circadian rhythm which is defined as a 24-hour repeating cycle of biochemical, physiological, or behavioral processes in a living organism; these in turn follow the patterns of the day/night cycle.

He pointed out that most people are aware that their body is doing "different things" when they are awake as compared to when they are asleep. By the way sleeping for up to 8 hours per night is a major component of a circadian rhythm. However, what following the *LifeWaves*® program demonstrates is that your body follows and creates a multitude of additional biochemical and physiological rhythms throughout the day and night. It is the interconnectedness of these rhythms to the larger circadian rhythm that creates health! More importantly, you can achieve a good measure of control over your body's rhythms.

What does being healthy mean?

Specifically, the circadian rhythm is the cycle of physiological processes which recur regularly over a 24-hour period. Body temperature, hormone secretion, modulation of the heartbeat, and respiration rate are all on a 24-hour cycle. These are the body's most basic functions. The quality of health of these cycles determines your overall health.

Health can be defined as the "coherent variability" of your physiology within the circadian rhythm. Put less formally, you are truly healthy when you sleep at night, are awake and alert during the day with your metabolism peaking in the afternoon.

This kind of health gives you the flexibility to face the stress in your life more effectively. For example, healthy individuals have the capacity to react to a stressful event or situation and then recover from it – to turn off the stress response when it is no longer needed. On the program this process is observed by looking at the acceleration and deceleration of the heartbeat.

How easy is it to turn off the stress response? Not so easy to accomplish because *the patterns of today's relentlessly high-pressure society are constantly training us to keep our stress response turned on.* Stress becomes our pattern of living, our pattern of existence. Repetition of this pattern teaches our physiology to be less variable. Lessened variability means that our stress reaction becomes flattened or less robust. Accordingly we lose the ability to recover from stress as well as the ability to turn off that stress reaction.

Further the cumulative effect of flattening of the variability is that the metabolism becomes de-linked from physical activity. In other words the various sub-systems of the body work more independently and less as a team. The result of this for PWPs is spasticity and hyper-reactivity. Tremors are an example of this process as this shaking continues when there is no external stimulus; there is a disconnect between the environment and the physiology.

The more variable your heart rate becomes the more precise and appropriate your physiological reactions to the environment become. The right amount of variability, at the right time, is health.

What happens during a session?

To observe and monitor heart rate variability, the program participant wears a Polar watch and belt with transmitter. The heart rate during a session is recorded and transmitted to the watch which is further uploaded to computer files and e-mailed to *LifeWaves®* for analysis. Based on a battery of analyses, individual sessions with the program participant are modified.

What *LifeWaves®* observes and acts upon is how we can change an unhealthy physiology by properly reacting to and recreating our heart wave patterns. These waves are the literal interpretation of the physiological responses that your body creates: reactions to stress and recovery, reactions to waking and sleeping, as well as all of your other behaviors. These reactions are "waves," and all physiological processes are composed of these "waves." Making the right "waves" at the right time, creates health.

As we look in on an exercise session remember that the exercise is not for physical conditioning in the traditional sense. The sets are designed for the specific purpose of reminding the body of how it functioned when it was healthy.

Basic equipment needed: stationary bicycle with movable arms and (optional) a set of stairs with at least 12 steps.

Definitions

Base-line heart beat: the heartbeat arrived at by sitting quietly for 5 minutes before the session begins. Deep breaths are taken periodically to further relax the physiology

Target heart rate: the heart rate that each cycle works toward; sometimes it is a specific number and sometimes it is expressed as a range. As a general rule, target heart rates increase for each cycle. The intervening targets increase according to your specific needs. All goals are set by target heart rate, not minimum time.

Rpms: this pedaling speed metric generally ranges from a low of 30 to a high of 60.

Recovery: generally a period of 3-5 minutes taken between cycles to ensure that the physiology relaxes as much as it is able during this timeframe. Whether or not you achieve an adequate recovery is judged by the resting heart rate, something the *LifeWaves*®Program teaches you to identify.

An example *LifeWaves*® Session.

It is important to note that every session is different. This example is offered as way to give you a flavor of what happens during a session.

Step 1 observe the heart beat for 5 minutes to establish a "base line" for the exercise session

Step 2a for the first cycle – pedal the stationary bike for a maximum of two minutes at the recommended exertion level and pattern. In this case, it was 10 seconds at 40 rpms with the goal of achieving the assigned target heart rate. Dismount from the bike and begin recovery

Step 2b recovery

Step 3a for the second cycle – pedal the stationary bike for 15 seconds at 50 rpms with the goal of achieving the assigned target heart rate, dismount from the bike and begin recovery

Step 3b same as 2b

Step 4a for the third cycle – pedal the stationary bike for 20 seconds at 60 rpms with a target heart rate, dismount from the bike and begin recovery

Step 4b same as 2b

Step 5a for the fourth cycle – pedal the stationary bike for 15 seconds at 50 rpms with a target heart rate of 20-25 above the baseline, dismount from the bike and begin recovery

Step 5b same as 2b

Step 6a for the fifth cycle – pedal the stationary bike for 10 seconds at 40 rpms with a target heart rate of 15-20 beats above the baseline, dismount from the bike and begin recovery

Step 6b recover – sit and wait for the heart rate to settle (about 7 minutes). Ideally the final resting heart rate will be higher than it was at the beginning of the cycles but not staying stuck at or near the target rate of the last cycle. Gradually the body remembers how to make the wave peak of activity followed by the trough of inactivity. For PWPs this means no longer "idling" at too high a rate. Much of the chronic fatigue for PWPs is due to our body engine idling on high most of the time.

This basic routine can be varied by asking that the cycles be done in 2-3 second bursts of energy within the total time target, e.g., if the total time of the cycle is 10 seconds, instead of accelerating to 40 rpms and staying there, pedal very fast, ease off, pedal fast again, ease off not exceeding 40 rpms over the 10 second periods. When plotted on a graph this shows a steeper curve of acceleration than is the case with the first example cycle.

An important tool called the "breath wave" is also frequently added to the program. This breathing exercise promotes heart rate variability and increases blood flow to the brain. Also from time to time going up and down stairs is substituted for one or two of the cycles using the bike.

While there are additional nuances to the program itself, I will not divert to a deeper technical discussion. Additional details can be found at www.lifewaves.com.

Additional eye witness reports

Lynne & Merrell Clark – longtime friends

Stan Smith has done remarkable things despite Parkinson's Disease. We think it was a miracle, but one that resulted from extremely hard work.

We saw Stan diminish dramatically when his PD was initially diagnosed. He and Roz bought a new home in the Southeast where living would be easier. When they visited us in Scarsdale, NY, we were happy to see old friends, but sad to see Stan still so diminished. More stooped, needed a cane for balance, found it difficult to climb stairs, walked with a shuffle. He needed help: with his coat, with food, carrying things.

He described his prognosis then as a downward series of plateaus, not up. But several years ago, the prognosis changed dramatically.

When we saw Stan recently he was much stronger than he had been before Parkinson's Disease. He walked erect, briskly, without shuffling and needed no cane. His grip was strong. His voice was strong. He was living a new life.

We have witnessed this hard won miracle, as if an eagle with a broken wing had healed and now was soaring higher than ever before.

Dr. Robert Frey – Chiropractor and Kinesiologist

Stan, you became my patient in 1997 about two years prior to your PD diagnosis. You've gone from deteriorating motor skills and liver and heart issues to improving motors skills, no liver chemistry problem and a "normal" heart examination.

Ellen Galinsky – business colleague

When I met Stan Smith in 2002, he had tremors in his hand and was walking slowly, stiffly, and hesitantly, using a cane to steady himself. In 2007, my organization (Families & Work Institute) honored Stan with a Work Life Legacy Award and although he was still walking with a cane, he was much more vigorous for all the events surrounding the honor. Three years later, the cane was gone and he could stand and walk for long periods of time. Today's Stan bears very little resemblance to the person I met long ago. Rather than Parkinson's progressing, it seems to be receding. It has been an amazing transformation.

Neale Godfrey – business colleague

I met Stan Smith over 7 years ago. During a first meeting, the obvious thing that strikes you about Stan is his brilliance and vision. He is a man who can see into the future of the workplace and into the needs of our next generation. In life, there are moments when you meet someone who can finish your sentences. Stan was one of those people. But, I could see that Stan's body was not keeping pace with his mind…it was holding him back.

His voice was tentative and without affect. His hands were trembling, he sort of shuffled along and dragged his feet. He said that he was also a singer, but really didn't do much singing anymore. He spoke of his voice in the past tense. Stan would dose-off in meetings.

Stan diligently follows the LifeWaves®Program. He does it on time and when and how he should. I think that may be one reason the effects are so dramatic. Stan is committed to his health. He is committed to not being his disease.

I have watched the transformation with both smiles and tears of joy. Stan, Roz and I have become dear friends. I have watched Stan go from walking with a cane and shuffle to walking with a gait which outpaces me. The cane is gone. Stan's broken voice is fixed…in all ways! He has written two books, cut a CD of show tunes and

Roz and I wept when he stood, yes stood, to sing a performance of Messiah.

Stan is a role model for all of us, certainly for me. Stan is truly committed to life.

Artie Maier – mentee

Stan has been a good friend and mentor of mine for over 15 years, and I've personally witnessed the incredible health transformation that he has achieved with the help of his doctor and his workout regime; it's been nothing short of inspirational to behold. Considering that Parkinson's is a progressive and degenerative disease, by all logic, it should get worse over time, but somehow, against all medical odds, Stan has found a way to make significant improvements in his quality of life through sheer willpower, sweat, and a positive mental attitude that just won't quit.

Years ago, before he started working out with the LifeWaves® Program, the physical symptoms of the disease were hard to miss. Stan and I would often go to lunch to talk about life and philosophy, and although I tried hard to ignore it, it was clear that he had trouble performing some seemingly simple tasks, like picking up silverware and navigating food into his mouth. The telltale "tremors" in his arm seemed to never stop. Walking and even speaking seemed to require a great deal of focus and effort, and as a result, I believe he learned how to choose his words carefully, because he simply did not have the energy to waste on rambling or nonsense. Our conversations were always thought-provoking and rich, and I was always impressed at how he always managed to stay positive and see the bright side of things, even when his condition took turns for the worse. I believe that positive attitude was perhaps the keystone of his transformation. It provided the fertile grounds required to sow the seeds of change and reap the benefits down the line.

Seeing him now, it's like a whole new Stan! After just a few years of working with his Doctor, he was able to walk around (without a cane), stand up, sit down, crack jokes, and generally move about with a sense of comfort and ease that I had never seen in him before. I can hear the difference in his voice; he speaks faster, with more energy, and without pause. He's always been passionate about his work, but now it seems like he has the energy to actually tackle the big problems. This has been by no means a cure for Stan. He still has Parkinson's, and he lives with it every day, but I'm happy see that this program has given him back somewhat of a "normal" lifestyle, and that's better than the best medicine on the market has to offer. I'm so happy for him, and hope he keeps up the good fight.

Gina Martindale – business colleague

I have known Stan Smith since I began working for him in 2007. Since that time, I have witnessed a complete physical metamorphosis. When I joined Stan's team, he struggled to put on his jacket without some additional assistance, walked with a cane and at times fought to maintain alertness throughout a meeting agenda. In fact, some of our team members would joke that if Stan could accomplish all he had done with Parkinson's, imagine all that he could do if he didn't have Parkinson's!

I have always admired Stan Smith and never doubted the power of his mind. However, I never imagined that I would witness the transformation that he was able to achieve in the years that I have known him. My most recent visit with Stan was a breakfast meeting where he met me out in the parking lot (sans cane) and walked at a pace where I followed him into the restaurant. I didn't help him with any doors, chairs or his jacket and he even finished eating his breakfast before me. He was as sharp as a tack and even demonstrated a light jog on our walk back to our cars. He is truly one of the most amazing souls that I have ever encountered and I am so lucky to call him a friend.

Scott Randall – business colleague

I first started working with Stan when he was a principal at Deloitte LLP. I was immediately impressed with Stan's vision and big picture ideas - and surprised that he would sometimes doze off in the middle of a meeting. As his condition progressed, Stan had problems walking. One day, after not having seen Stan for some time, we had a particularly vibrant meeting and walked Stan to the lobby where he proceeded to practically bound down the stairs to the street level! What a sight to see! Stan really put his mind to what he could do and made it happen. Hooray!

Phillip Roark – business colleague

I first met Stan Smith in November 2000. We worked together on projects for nearly a decade after that date and we are still good friends today. From the time we met it was obvious that Stan was having some sort of symptoms that impacted his daily professional function especially alertness from time to time. Regardless, he was still a vibrant leader and quick thinker. Over the next few years, during our frequent interactions, it was more apparent he was in a type of decline physically. I was concerned for him. His mobility, and especially his quickness of movement changed dramatically.

However, to my surprise and relief this decline slowed. A type of stability appeared around 2006/7. Since then, he gradually overcame and started to manage and control his symptoms, walking independently and gaining an improved level of health and activity. Writing, singing, speaking, traveling, consulting and being in demand – 12 years later he is an active civic leader, mentor, successful author, businessman and husband.

Megan Turk – business colleague

I have known Stan since 2008. As the partner in charge of my group, he never faltered in his mental ability to lead and drive work, but Parkinson's at times brought him to a dead stop physically. Stan never complained, but the disease forced him to decline work travel and speaking opportunities because of the side effects. I was so inspired to see the video of him at a fast walk, cane free! He never gave up and made it happen for himself and his community. Amazing!

Jim Wall – business colleague

Stan and I have been colleagues and friends for over 15 years. When he was first diagnosed with Parkinson's Disease, we feared the worst and prayed for his recovery and rejuvenation of his body and his spirit. Over the past 6 years, we have seen just that! Gone are many of the symptoms of the disease. Stan's mobility, intellectual sharpness, confidence and sense of optimism and hope have all returned. While his struggle continues, he is a shining example of the power of determination, persistence and faith.

Stewart Watts – mentee

Stan has been a mentor of mine for well over a decade. Seeing Stan today, when I think back to the low points of his battle with Parkinson's, the memories hardly seem to be credible. Through those times and better times, he has remained dedicated to mastering the illness, as well as his body and mind. Beyond simply stalling the disease, Stan is as sharp and stable now as I have seen him in years.

Jim Wexler – business colleague

One knows immediately that Stan Smith is an idea man. We met many years ago in his role as accountancy/innovator at a Big 4 firm. It's not a typo and not an oxymoron with Stan Smith. He has been instrumental in using both sides of his brain to help these in-the-box guys think out. He'll master the granularity of a business transaction and sing show tunes with professional flair on the same afternoon. Together, we framed a way for the Big 4 accounting firm to become more relevant to the next generation workforce. The bulb that illuminated on this challenge for Stan: Make videogames that engaged them to learn, and overlay assessment criteria that measured them, and build a social relationship with them from the experience.

This was almost a decade ago, before multiplayer game deployments, before Facebook, and the idea was so advanced that today it appears shockingly fresh. So for his big brain to have its wiring go haywire was a tremendous loss, for those he touched and those he served. Stan started to need a cane. He'd slip away from a brilliant thought in mid-sentence, appear to doze, and then awaken and complete it. It was bizarre, worrisome, and potentially tragic. So, of course, Stan thought out of the box he was in, and found a way to rewire his essence, his mortal coil. Amazing, unprecedented, but not surprising at all with Stan Smith. We all love you Stan.

Marlene & Joe Zakierski – longtime friends

Stan and his lovely wife, Roz are our dear family friends who we have had the pleasure of knowing during the last 25 years. When Stan first became ill, it was sad to see how this vibrant man was becoming more and more debilitated as each month passed.

When Stan and Roz moved to South Carolina, he began an intensive program under the guidance of trainers from LifeWaves®. Of course, knowing Stan's perseverance and hearing his faith in his doctor's protocol, we held our breath and looked forward to an improvement in Stan's strength, walking ability, speech and overall return to his youthful demeanor.

Stan makes several trips to New York each year and on occasion he and Roz have been our houseguests. During these visits, it seemed as if a miracle had occurred! There seemed to be a total transformation in his walking, speech and range of motion. It has been incredible to witness the return of his strength and stamina.

This major improvement can only be attributed to Stan's ardent adherence to the LifeWaves®Cycles Exercise® Program and Stan's determination and positive attitude.

About the Authors

W. Stanton Smith is a Person With Parkinson's (PWP) having been diagnosed in 1999. He is the Vice-President of the Parkinsons Support Group of the Upstate, a registered 501(c)3 not for profit and member of the advisory committee to the Neurology Department of the Greenville Hospital System. His wife, Roz, is his Care Partner (CP). They have been married for over 33 years and reside in the Greenville, SC area.

They are partners in W. Stanton Smith LLC which publishes Stan's books. They are both members of the Westminster Presbyterian Church of Greenville, SC and its Sanctuary Choir. Roz and Stan actively support the Greenville Symphony Orchestra (GSO), and are members of the Guild of the GSO of which Roz is an officer.

For nearly 30 years Roz worked as a senior professional in the marketing research business working on major global brands. She lived in Washington D.C. and Rome, Italy as a child. She spent her teen years in the Poughkeepsie, NY area and attended the Oakwood Friends School. She holds bachelors and masters degrees from Cornell University.

Stan was in the business world for 36+ years. For most of his career he served in senior Human Resources positions with professional services firms. He was born and raised in Houston, Texas. He received a B.S. in Economics from the Wharton School, University of Pennsylvania, and an MBA from the University of Texas at Austin. Professionally he is a recognized expert in intergenerational communication issues in the workplace.

In November 2010 Stan Smith published his second book, *Decoding Generational Differences: Changing your mindset...Without losing your mind.* In this book Stan expands on extensive research conducted during the previous decade to help executives, parents, and teachers understand gen y and how to effectively communicate with this new generation in the workplace.

Recently Stan introduced an interactive presentation to help young people work more effectively with bosses from older generations. In early 2012 he began writing a column called "Ask the Boss" which is part of a college-directed website collegebuzzz.com. His book *Ask the Boss: 101 Tips for Success (even if you don't have a job yet)* will be published in the spring of 2012 by W. Stanton Smith LLC.

All Stan's books are available from www.wstantonsmith.com.